To: From:

On the occasion of:

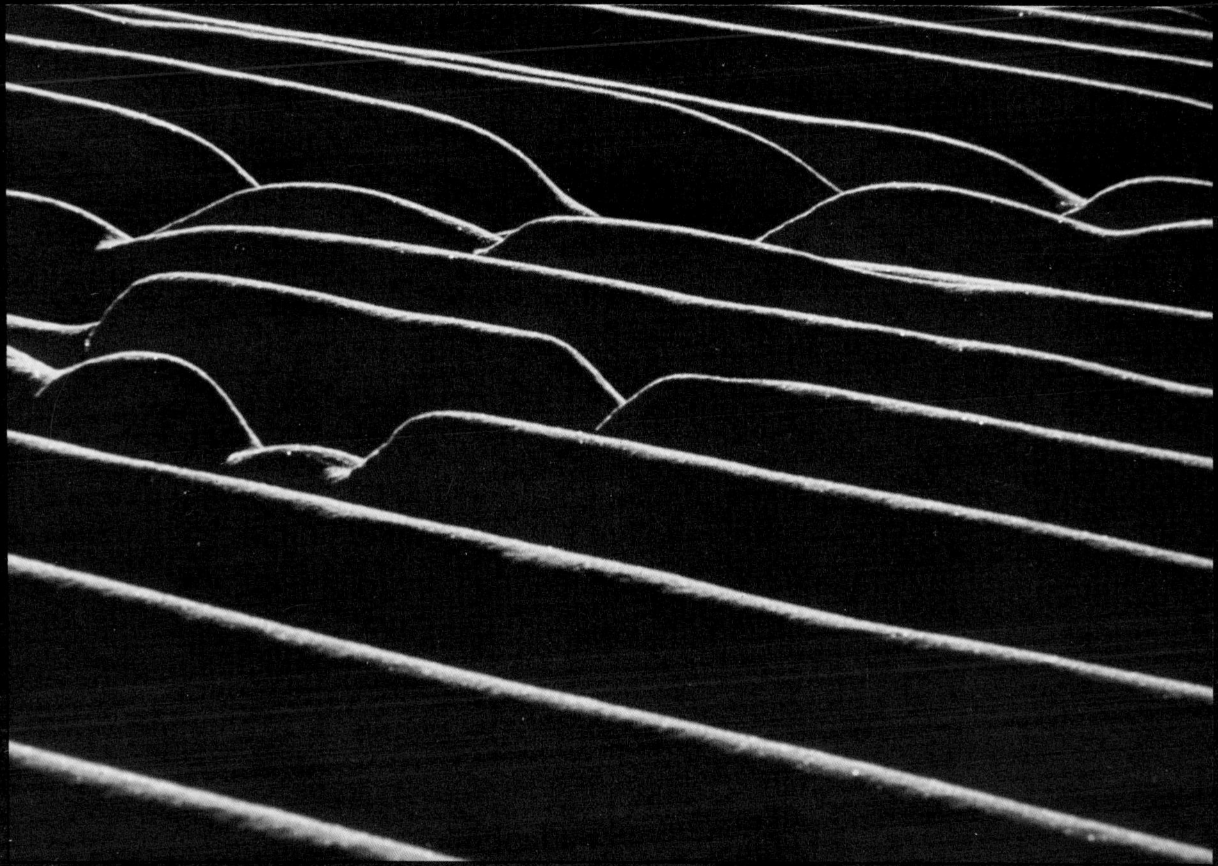

SONG OF CREATION

By Cyril A. Reilly

Winston Press

Cover Design: Studio One
Interior Design: Miriam Frost

©1983 by Cyril A. Reilly All rights reserved.
Printed in the United States of America 5 4 3 2 1
ISBN: 0-86683-629-2 Library of Congress Cat. Card Number: 82-62815
Winston Press Inc., 430 Oak Grove, Minneapolis, MN 55403

In the beginning, all the world was darkness;
God's spirit hovered above the empty waters.

Then in His love He said,
"I want the light to shine."
Light was everywhere!

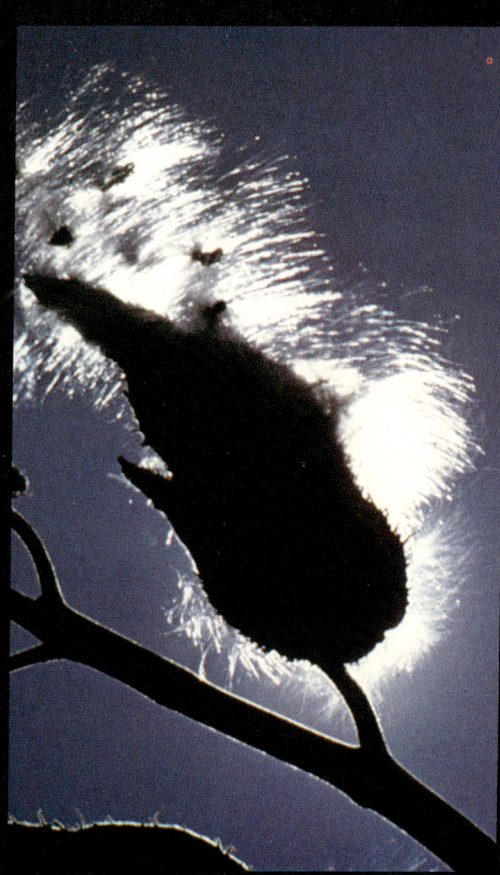

Father, thank you for the light you give to us:

Sunlight, moonlight—every light is you.

14

God made the earth:

plains and mighty mountains,

valleys and meadows and
trees that touch the sky;

22

flowers and fruits,

and all that walks
or creeps or flies—

26

and He found it good.

Father, thank you for this earth you give to us;

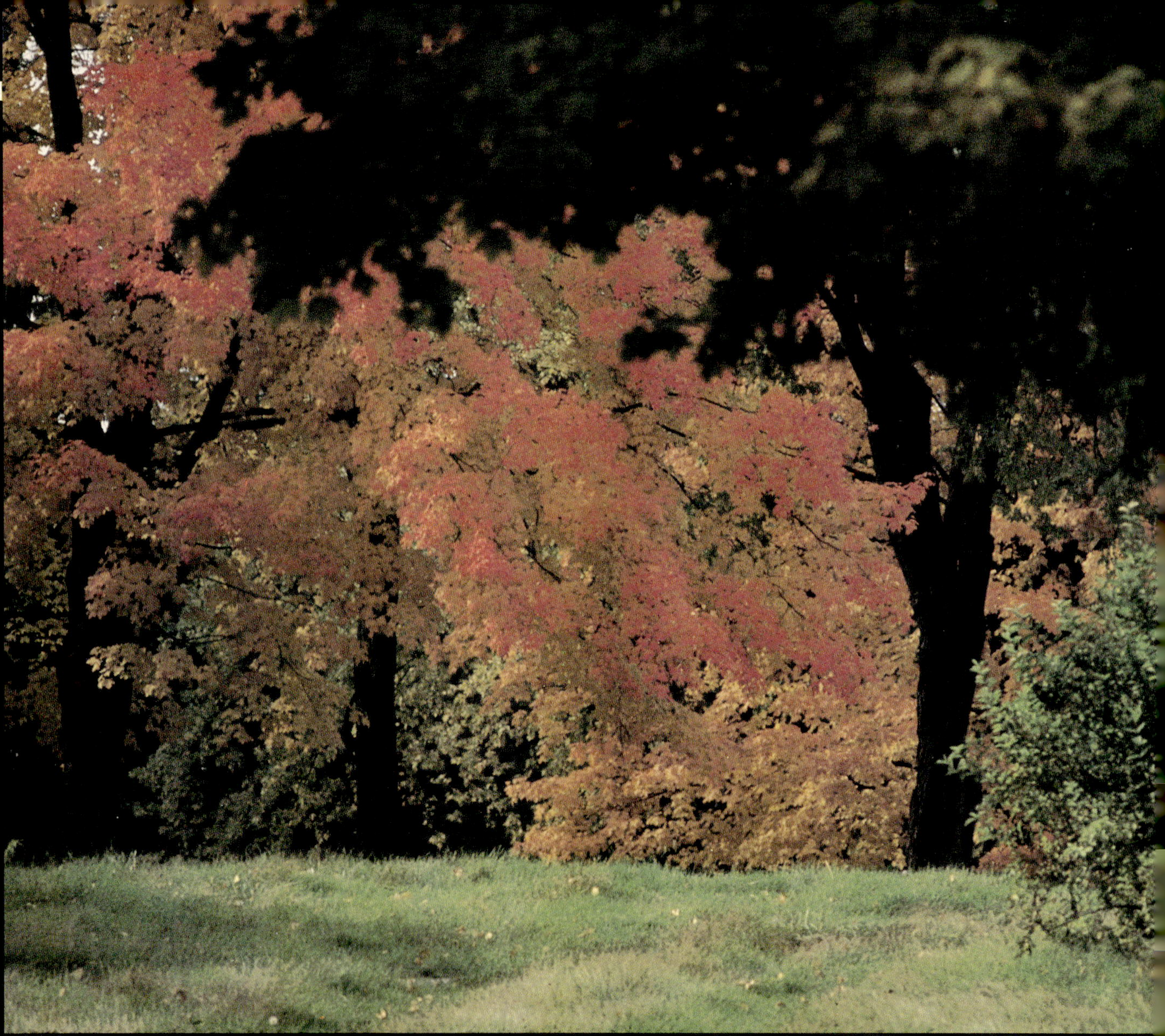

life and beauty . . .

. . . shine out everywhere.

God made the waters: swiftly rushing rivers, blue misty lakes . . .

37

. . . and the never resting oceans;

39

40

filled them with life, with mystery and majesty — and He found them good.

42

43

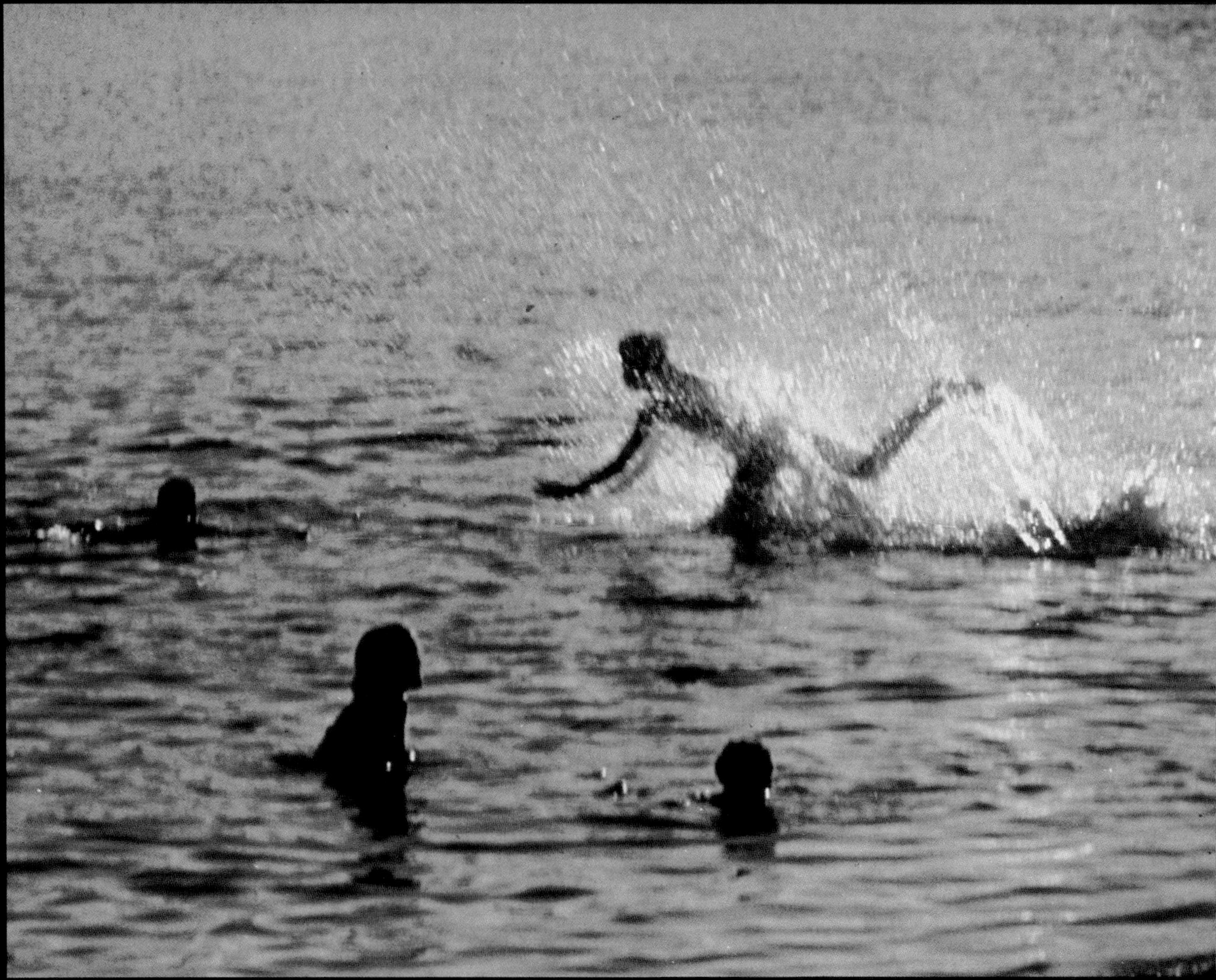

Father, thank you for the waters you have made:

flowing waters bring us back to you.

47

God made man and woman, filled them
with His God-life; called them His own,
made them masters of creation;

49

told them to love and praise
the wonders God had done—
then and evermore.

51

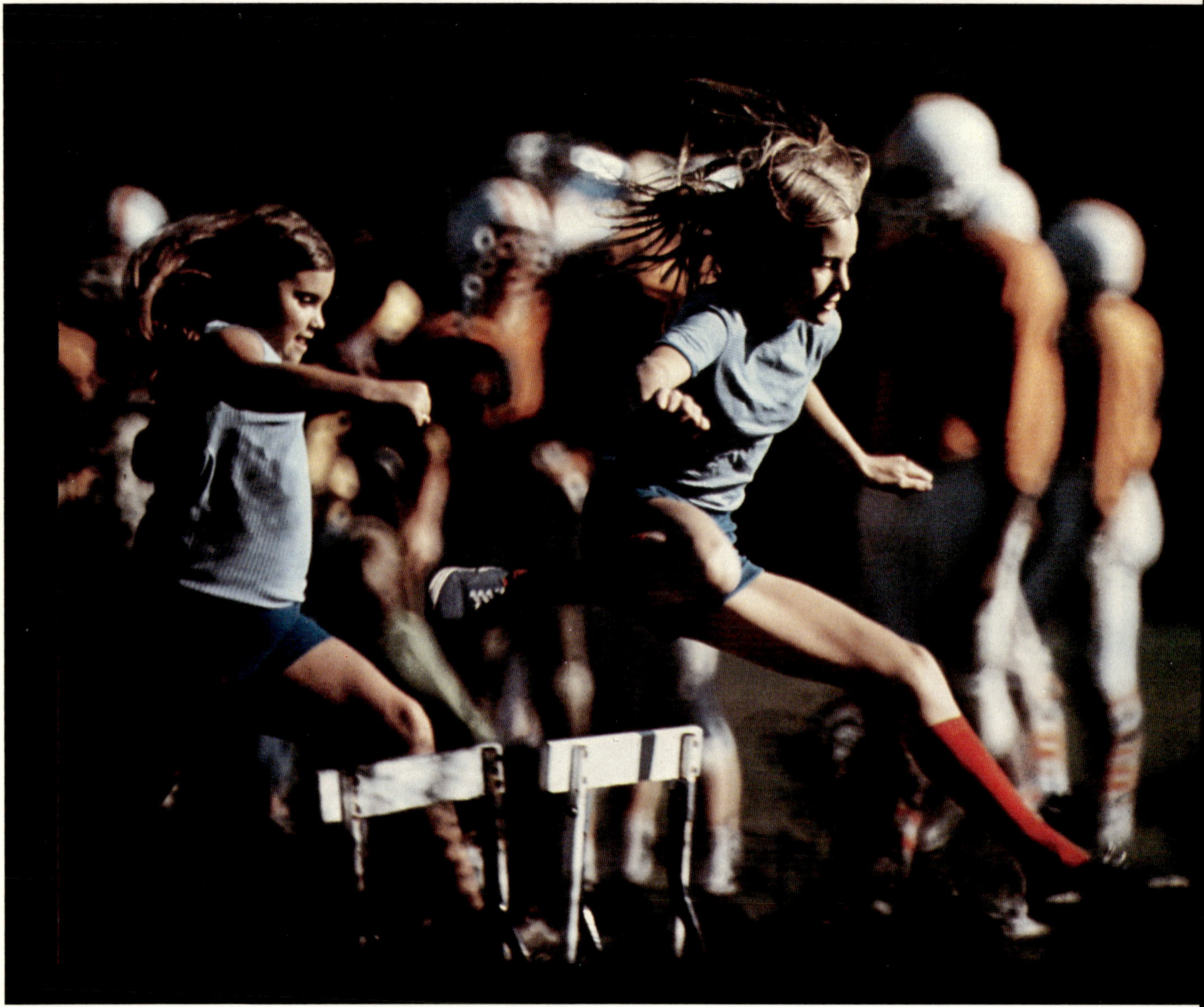

Father, thank you for this life you give to us,

54

for creation . . .

. . . and a voice to sing.

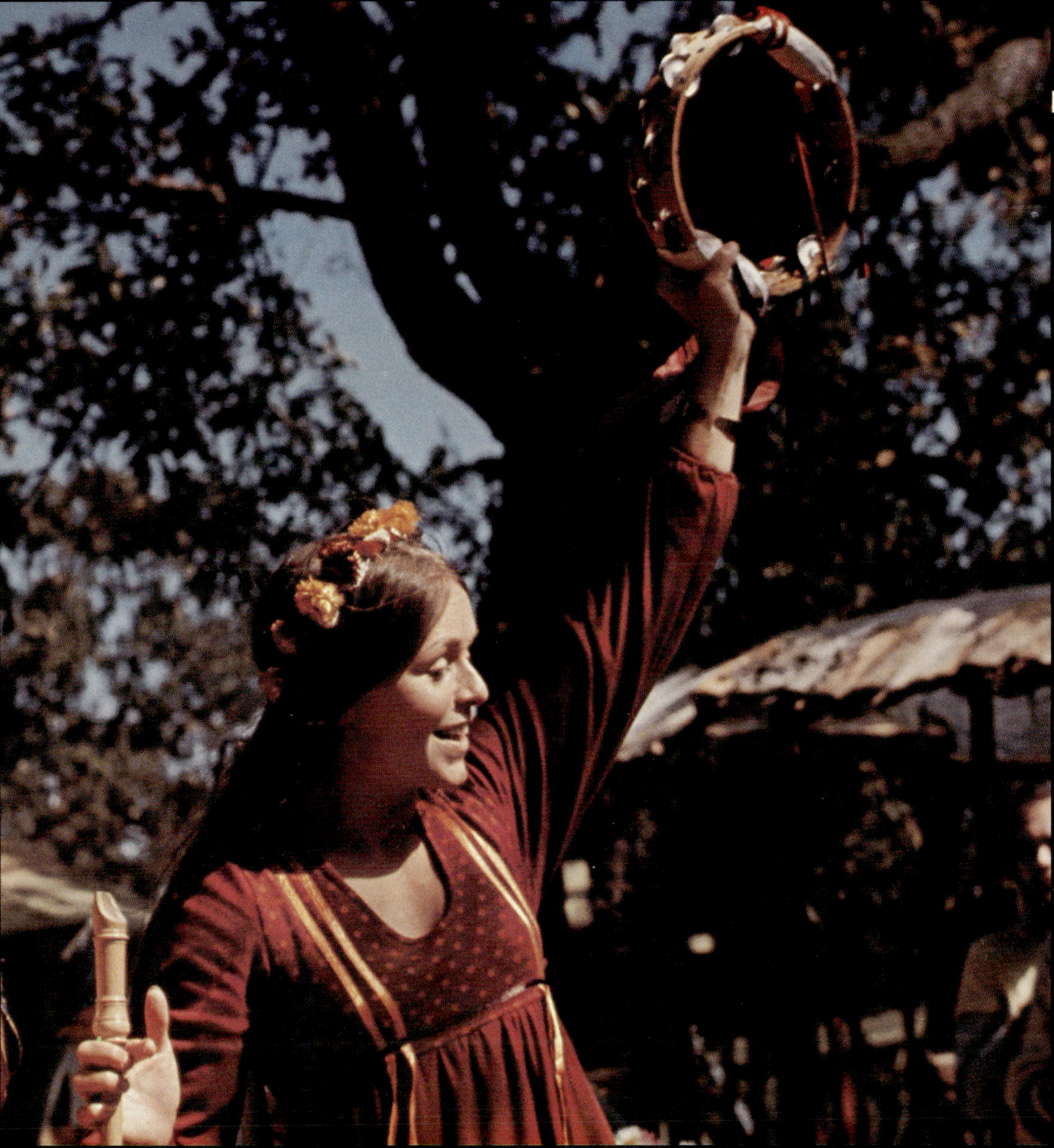

When thistles grew
in an empty garden,
God's only Son died and rose
and taught His people:

now bread and wine
and coins and sparrows
led to God—

59

60

we could see once more!

62

Father, thank you—
Christ your light is shining now:
In His brightness all the world is new.

64